Navajo Weaving Today

Nancy N. Schiffer

Schiffer Publishing Ltd

1469 Morstein Road, West Chester, Pennsylvania 19380

Title page photo:
Pastel vegetal dyed wool weaving. Woven by Lillian Joe, Burntwater, 1990. 47" x 37". Courtesy, Foutz Trading Company.

Photos this page:
Two contemporary saddle blankets popularly called "Gallup throws", 1990. Each 38½" x 19½". Courtesy Schiffer Publishing Collection.

Photographs of landscapes on Navajo lands by H.L. James. Photographs of the objects by Douglas Congdon-Martin, Herbert N. Schiffer and Peter N. Schiffer.

Copyright © 1991 by Schiffer Publishing, Ltd.
Library of Congress Catalog Number: 90-60957.

Printed in the United States of America.
ISBN: 0-88740-319-0

We are interested in hearing from authors with book ideas on related topics.

Published by Schiffer Publishing, Ltd.
1469 Morstein Road
West Chester, Pennsylvania 19380
Please write for a free catalog.
This book may be purchased from the publisher.
Please include $2.00 postage.
Try your bookstore first.

CONTENTS

Pictorial weaving of lambs by Jane Gray, 1990. 23¼″ x 22″. Courtesy, Schiffer Publishing Collection.

Cotton ready for spinning into the strong supporting weaving strands. Courtesy, Foutz Trading Company.

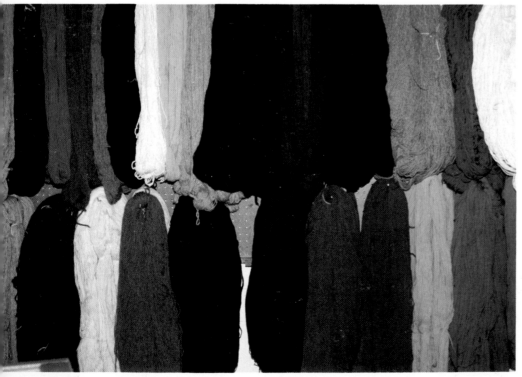

Dyed wool yarn ready for weaving the decorative designs. Courtesy, Foutz Trading Company.

INTRODUCTION

The Pueblo inhabitants along the Rio Grande River in northern New Mexico were weaving cotton before the arrival of Spanish sheep in the sixteenth century. Into this arid and mountainous land the Navajo people migrated and learned to weave from their new neighbors. Early weavings are so rare that mere traces of original patterns exist to tell us little of the size or uses of the cloths. But by the time white people contacted the Navajo they were proficient at weaving blankets with horizontal bands of natural and vegetal dyed colors.

As the United States expanded into the Southwest during the nineteenth century, examples of high quality Navajo weavings were recorded. Blankets were either "finely woven and thin (famous for being waterproof,) or soft and loosely woven. There was very little weaving of the middle quality." (Rodee, 1987, p. 65.) The blankets became trade items and when the system of traders became established at the end of the century, the weavers were encouraged to make heavier goods to be sold in the East as rugs, not blankets.

Geometric patterns in wool left natural or dyed with vegetal, mineral, or commercial analin dyes have developed around the regional trading posts. Here the weavers both exchanged their work for goods and were encouraged by the traders who often introduced different materials and design ideas. The evolution of designs is on-going in the living art of weaving.

Oil on canvas painting of a loom and weaving tools. Painted by Bea Diclo, 1989. 24" x 30". Courtesy, Shiprock Trading Company.

Upright loom used by the Navajo.
This miniature is for small weavings
and demonstration of the weaving
process. 14⅜" x 15½". Courtesy,
Private Collection.

Contemporary weaving, "Gallup
throw" style, 1990. 38½" x 19½".
Courtesy, Schiffer Publishing
Collection.

Two contemporary weavings used as pillow covers and woven in a general style in the area north of Gallup, New Mexico. 11" x 12". Courtesy, Schiffer Publishing Collection.

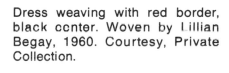

Dress weaving with red border, black center. Woven by Lillian Begay, 1960. Courtesy, Private Collection.

Red dress weaving of the traditional Navajo style, circa 1960. Courtesy, Dennehotso Collection.

Three Turkey type, Burntwater style weaving in vegetal dyed wool. Woven by Helen Bia, Three Turkey, Arizona. 24″ x 36″. Courtesy, Hubbell Trading Post.

Burntwater style weaving with a border. Woven by Mary Lee Begay, Ganado, Arizona. 37″ x 59″. Courtesy, Keams Canyon Arts and Crafts.

REGIONAL STYLES

Burntwater

The most recent area to develope a whole new style of weaving is around Burntwater, Arizona. Here, in 1968, a weaver took the risk of making an all-vegetal dyed geometric rug with a border. The rug sold right away (James, 1988, p. 77) and the trader encouraged the weaver and others to continue the practice. Borrowing design elements from Ganado and Two Grey Hills styles, they developed beautifully woven rugs. In the early 1980s, traders Bruce Burnham at Sanders, Arizona and Bill Malone at Ganado, Arizona continued to encourage the development of the Burntwater style which by then was recognised as a distinct type. Adding to its intricate construction has been the use of Wide Ruins type horizontal bands, and the use of commercial yarns in unusual soft colors. The colors are achieved with plant materials such as wild sunflower seeds (aqua), mistletoe (dark aqua), mountain mahogany bark (brown), cedar root (pink), and black walnut skins (beige), among many others.

Vegetal dyed handspun wool weaving in Burntwater style, from the late 1960s. 36" x 60". Courtesy, Keams Canyon Arts and Crafts.

Vegetal dyed Burntwater style weaving. 37" x 54". Courtesy, Keams Canyon Arts and Crafts.

Burntwater combination style weaving of Wide Ruins horizontal bands interrupted by a Two Grey Hills geometric pattern, all vegetal dyed commercial wool. Woven by Susie Small Canyon. 41″ x 32½″. Courtesy, Hogback Trading Post.

Burntwater style weaving of geometric design, 1990. Woven by Susie Smallcanyon. 41″ x 32½″. Courtesy, Hogback Trading Post.

Central vegetal design, Burntwater style weaving. Woven by Virginia Bia, Burntwater, Arizona, 1990. 59″ x 44″. Courtesy, Hubbell Trading Post.

Burntwater style all-vegetal dyed weaving, 1990. Woven by Elsie Bia, Burntwater, Arizona. 34" x 54". Courtesy, Hubbell Trading Post.

Burntwater style geometric weaving with bands at two ends. Woven by Nellie Joe. 34½" x 32½". Courtesy, Foutz Trading Company.

Small blue indigo dyed weaving of Burntwater style. Woven by Arlene John, Burntwater, Arizona, 1990. 33½" x 26". Courtesy, Kiva Indian Trading Post.

Burntwater pastel weaving of geometric design. Woven by Mary Lee Begay, Ganado, Arizona, 1990. 36″ x 60″. Courtesy, Hubbell Trading Post.

Brown and light blue geometric designed rug in Burntwater style. Woven by Della Yazzie, Burntwater, Arizona, 1990. 53″ x 43″. Courtesy, Kiva Indian Trading Post.

Weaving with two diamonds design in Burntwater style with a Wide Ruins type band at each end. 59″ x 35½″. Courtesy, Foutz Trading Company.

Pastel geometric designed weaving, Burntwater style. Woven by Wande Tracey. Courtesy, Foutz Trading Company.

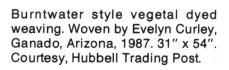

Burntwater style vegetal dyed weaving. Woven by Evelyn Curley, Ganado, Arizona, 1987. 31″ x 54″. Courtesy, Hubbell Trading Post.

Combination Burntwater style weaving with corn plant tree of life with bird design superimposed on Wide Ruins style bands. Woven by Susie Smallcanyon, 1990. 41¼″ x 31¼″. Courtesy, Hogback Trading Post.

Burntwater style weaving in all figured bands. Woven by Nettie Nelson, Burntwater, Arizona, 1990. 43″ x 64″. Courtesy, Hubbell Trading Post.

Wide Ruins

The modern Wide Ruins style of Navajo weaving developed around 1940 in the environs of the Wide Ruins Trading Post which now is a ruin itself but which stood near route 191 south of Ganado, Arizona.

The style is characterized by a borderless field of horizontal bands with stepped diamonds and contrasting colors which may resemble a zipper pattern. The colors are achieved with natural and vegetal dyed wool.

Miniature weaving in Wide Ruins style with natural wool in figured bands. 17" x 11½". Courtesy, Foutz Trading Company.

Wide Ruins style weaving with vegetal dyed colors and natural white wool. Woven by Manie Kit. 34" x 59". Courtesy, Keams Canyon Arts and Crafts.

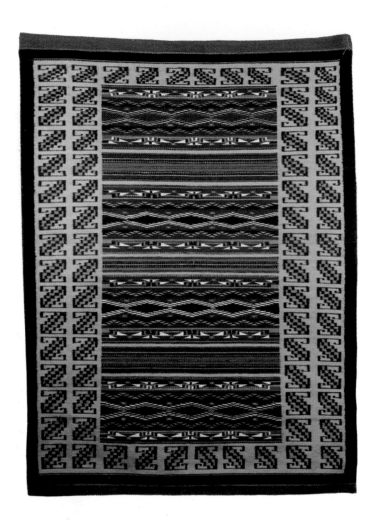

Opposite page, top left:
Wide Ruins style weaving with an unusual blue figured border design. Woven by Cora and Leonard Goody, Wide Ruins, Arizona. 51½" x 38". Courtesy, Hogback Trading Company.

Bottom left:
Wide Ruins style weaving of exceptionally fine quality. Woven by Brenda Spencer. 30" x 42". Courtesy, Hubbell Trading Post.

Top right:
Wide Ruins style weaving with interesting colors. Woven by Irene Begay, Wide Ruins, Arizona. 41". Courtesy, Hogback Trading Post.

Bottom right:
Wide Ruins style weaving, circa 1989. 29" x 42". Courtesy, Keams Canyon Arts and Crafts.

This page right:
Pastel shades in horizontal stripes on this Wide Ruins style weaving with an unusual black border. Woven by Cora Gaddy, Wide Ruins, Arizona. 63" x 45". Courtesy, Hogback Trading Post.

Below:
Wide Ruins style weaving with an unusual Ganado influence in the dark red, grey, and white design. Woven by Mary Baldwin, Wide Ruins, Arizona. 25" x 37". Courtesy, Hubbell Trading Post.

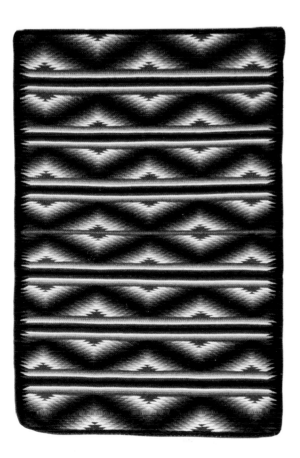

Wide Ruins bands. Woven by Betty Roan, St. Michaels. 42" x 35". Courtesy, Foutz Trading Company.

Oil on canvas, painting of a group of people playing cards in the shade of a summer shelter. Shown on the ground is a blanket in the chief style. Painted by William Hatch, circa 1980. Courtesy, Dennehotso Collection.

First Phase Chief blanket. Woven by Sadie Curtis, Ganado, Arizona, 1990. 58" x 57". Courtesy, Hubbell Trading Post.

Ganado

The trading post at Ganado, Arizona has been in existence since 1871 serving the local Navajo population. It is found off Route 264 near Route 291 in northeastern Arizona. The post's most celebrated owner was Juan Lorenzo Hubbell who was very influential in the development of the regional weaving style in that area after he acquired the post in 1878. Not only did he, and his manager C. N. Cotton, develope a thriving business in Navajo rugs, he also commissioned watercolor paintings of older rug patterns to be made to hang in his post and serve as models for the weavers. (See them all reproduced in Rodee, 1987, pages 91-97.) The paintings are still on display on the rug room wall. The post has been a U. S. National Park Service National Historic Site since 1967.

The typical Ganado style has a black outside border with strong geometric patterns in natural grey and white and commercially dyed red and black wool. Revivals of older Ganado styles continue to be made and are popular trade pieces.

Third Phase Chief's blanket. Woven by Marlene White, Ganado, Arizona, 1990. 47" x 49". Courtesy, Hubbell Trading Post.

Third Phase Chief's blanket, 1989. 48" x 48". Courtesy, Keams Canyon Arts and Crafts.

Copy of an old design, blue, Ganado style. Woven by Rose Bighouse, circa 1970. Courtesy, Dennehotso Collection.

Old classic Ganado style weaving with red background. Woven by Lenora Begay, Ganado, Arizona, 1990. 25″ X 37″. Courtesy, Hubbell Trading Post.

Ganado old style weaving by Jessie Harvey, 1989. 64″ x 48″. Courtesy, Foutz Trading Post.

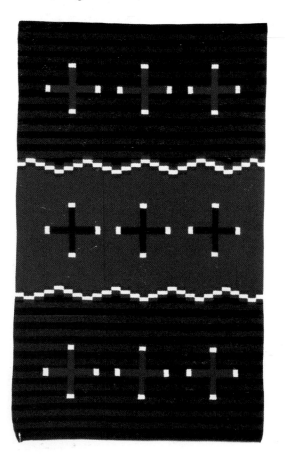

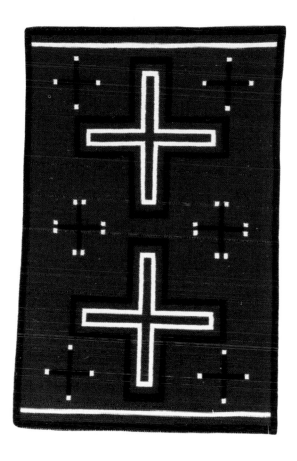

Ganado old style weaving by Mary Lee Begay, Ganado, Arizona, 1990. 24″ x 40″. Courtesy, Hubbell Trading Post.

Ganado old style weaving by Nellie Klade, Chinle, Arizona, 1990. 28″ x 50″. Courtesy, Hubbell Trading Post.

Red weaving with no border, Ganado old style. Woven by Genene Tsinajinnie, Ganado, Arizona, 1990. 62″ x 48″. Hubbell Trading Post.

Ganado style weaving with predominant geometric design and border, 1990. 60½" x 37". Courtesy, Hubbell Trading Post.

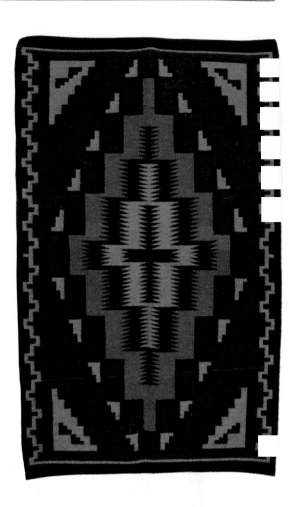

Classic Ganado red weaving with central stepped diamond pattern and border. Woven by Pauline Nez, Hogback, circa 1980. Courtesy, Dennehotso Collection.

Weaving in reproduction of Ganado Germantown design with a border. Woven by Sally Scott, 1990. Courtesy, Foutz Trading Company.

Geometric, hand spun and carded weaving in Ganado style. Woven by Ann Shirley, 1990. 48½" x 37¼". Courtesy, Turquoise Lady.

Ganado red and white weaving with corn plant design in rows. This design combines the Wide Ruins influence of bands with Ganado colors and the pictorial corn plant. Woven by Ruby Eltel. 47" x 34". Courtesy, Turquoise Lady.

Ganado style weaving with natural grey wool background. 39" x 61". Courtesy, Keams Canyon Arts and Crafts.

Ganado red weaving of geometric symmetry. Woven by Mae Curley, Ganado, Arizona. 33" x 45". Courtesy, Hubbell Trading Post.

Ganado red weaving. 38″ x 53″. Courtesy, Keams Canyon Arts and Crafts.

Ganado red weaving. 36″ x 60″. Courtesy, Keams Canyon Arts and Crafts.

Ganado red pattern with plain black border. 36″ x 57″. Courtesy, Keams Canyon Arts and Crafts.

Unusual Ganado style cross weaving with yellow, red, and black. Woven by Sylvia Shay, Pinon, Arizona, 1989. Courtesy, Hubbell Trading Post.

Ganado red design and a tree of life with bird design in a new style combination weaving. Woven by Priscilla Tsinajinnie, Cedar Ridge, Arizona. 30" x 56". Courtesy, Hubbell Trading Post.

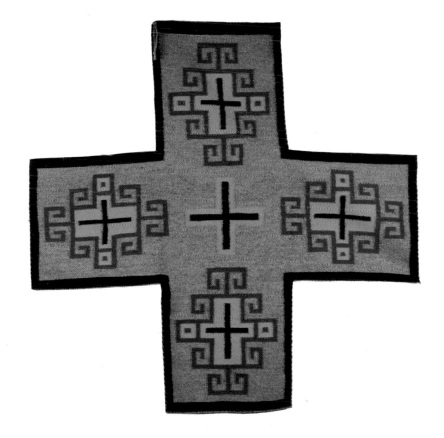

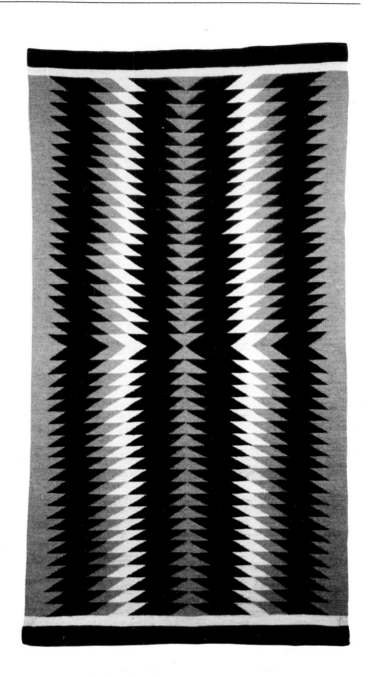

Lines of trapezoids in a black border, Klagetoh area, circa 1970. 82" x 54". Courtesy, Private Collection on permanent loan to Ohio University.

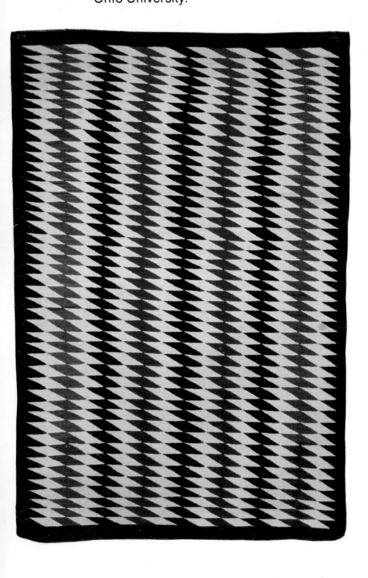

Klagetoh red style weaving. Woven by Lucy Benally, Klagetoh. 32" x 60". Courtesy, Hubbell Trading Post.

Crystal

John B. Moore started trading with the Navajos at Crystal, New Mexico, on the western slope of the Chuska mountains, in 1896. From here he inspired local weavers to make rugs sufficient to fill orders for his mail-order catalogs published in 1903 and 1911. (See reprint of them by Avanyu Publishing, 1987.) The bordered designs with geometric patterns have been highly influential to the present-day, especially to the Two Grey Hills area weavers.

Since the 1940s, a new Crystal style has developed of vegetal dyed horizontal bands including variegated "wavy" zones and no border. The golden tones of these rugs have made them distinctive among Navajo weavings.

Woven mat in a design based on early Crystal weavings. 17½" x 15". Courtesy, Foutz Trading Company.

J.B. Moore style weaving based on the early 20th century published designs. Woven by Mary A. Ben, Klagetoh. 32" x 40". Courtesy, Hubbell Trading Post.

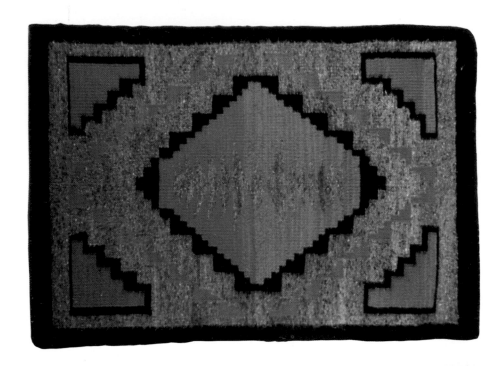

Small weaving based on early Crystal styles. Woven by Betty Joe, Red Valley. 22" x 31". Courtesy, Keams Canyon Arts and Crafts.

Crystal style weaving. 36" x 64". Courtesy, Keams Canyon Arts and Crafts.

Crystal style weaving with bold geometric design, circa 1950. Courtesy, Dewey Galleries, Ltd.

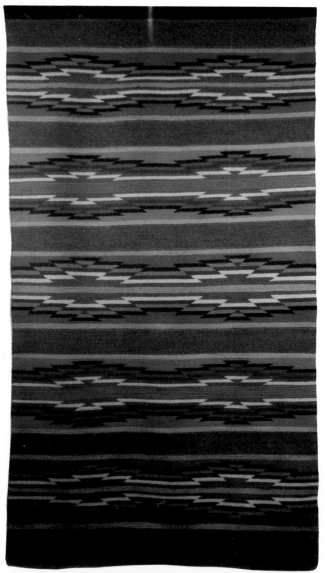

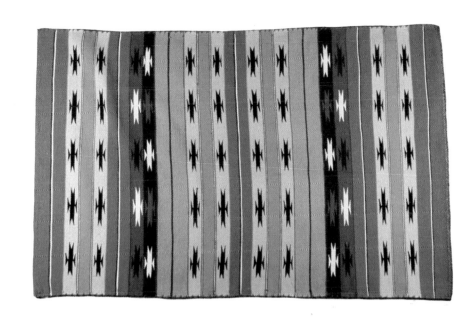

Crystal style weaving of hand carded and spun wool. Woven by Virginia Begay. 47½" x 30". Courtesy, Turquoise Lady.

Crystal style weaving with bands of mixed lines, yellow tones. Woven by Alice Begay, Crystal, New Mexico. 29" x 50". Courtesy, Hubbell Trading Post.

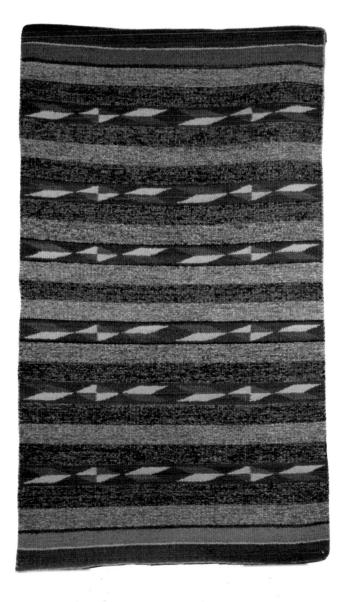

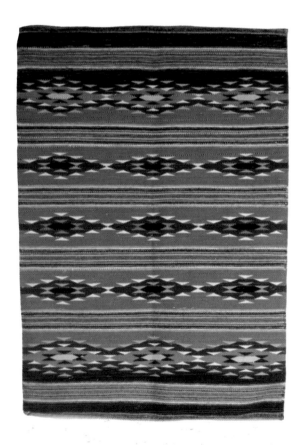

Crystal style weaving. Woven by Geniva Shabi. Courtesy, Keams Canyon Arts and Crafts.

Miniature weaving in Crystal style with black border. Woven by Daisy Kee. 6½" x 4". Courtesy, Private Collection.

Crystal style weaving. Woven by Joan Kee, Teec Nos Pos. 56" x 37". Courtesy, Foutz Trading Company.

Crystal style weaving, red and brown stripes. Woven by Lucy Tsosie, Crystal, New Mexico. 55" x 36". Courtesy, Hogback Trading Post.

Miniature weaving of Crystal style. Woven by Susie Bia. Courtesy, Hubbell Trading Post.

Miniature weaving of Crystal style. Courtesy, Adobe Gallery.

Crystal style weaving of fine quality. Woven by Grace Denetso, Crystal. 47" x 64". Courtesy, Hubbell Trading Post.

Chinle

The borderless horizontal bands of classic Navajo rugs inspired the modern Chinle weaving style which developed in the 1930s in the Canyon de Chelly region of northeastern Arizona. Here a few small trading posts competed for the Navajo's trade, including that of "Cozy" McSparron and his wife. Mrs. McSparron and others encouraged the local weavers to develop vegetal dyes and to improve the quality of weaving in the area. The beautiful bands which resulted, today including some commercially dyed details, alternate solid colors and stepped diamond patterns.

Recent weavings may include the raised outline technique which first developed on the far western areas of the Navajo reservation.

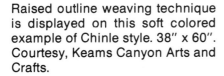

Raised outline weaving technique is displayed on this soft colored example of Chinle style. 38" x 60". Courtesy, Keams Canyon Arts and Crafts.

Chinle style weaving with three bands of stepped diamonds. Woven by Elizabeth Endischee. Courtesy, Foutz Trading Company.

Miniature weaving in the Chinle style. 5″ x 4″. Courtesy, Private Collection.

Chinle style weaving of vegetal dyed wool. Woven by Elouise Jones, Chinle. Courtesy, Hubbell Trading Post.

Chinle style weaving. Woven by Rose Bitsuie, Chinle. 33″ x 59″. Courtesy, Hubbell Trading Post.

Two Grey Hills

The rug catalogs published by John B. Moore at Crystal Trading Post in 1903 and 1911 most probably influenced the weavers on the opposite side of the Chuska mountains who developed the Two Grey Hills style. Near Route 666 in western New Mexico, where the Two Grey Hills Trading Post used to be, there developed a tradition of strong geometric patterns woven with finely carded natural white, grey and brown wool with some dyed black wool for details and the border. The weaving is characteristically of fine quality. Recently, more commercial wool has been used. Although the old post is gone now, the weavers continue the style and trade at other nearby posts.

Two Grey Hills style weaving. Woven by Elizabeth Nathaniel. 34" x 36". Courtesy, Foutz Trading Company.

Typical Two Grey Hills style weaving with commercial yarn, 1990. 43" x 30". Courtesy, Foutz Trading Company.

Two Grey Hills style weaving in natural wool. Woven at Hubbell Trading Post by Evelyn Curley, 1989. 36″ x 58″. Courtesy, Hubbell Trading Post.

Weaving with small geometric elements borrowed from Teec Nos Pos style designs. Woven by Cynthia Kellywood, Two Grey Hills. 24″ x 30″. Courtesy, Hubbell Trading Post.

Small mat of Two Grey Hills design style in natural colors of handspun wool. Woven by Eleanor Houge. 15″ x 23″. Courtesy, Dennehotso Collection.

Two Grey Hills style weaving, 1989.
36″ x 60″. Courtesy, Keams Canyon
Arts and Crafts.

Two Grey Hills style weaving.
Woven by Sherman. 60″ x 37″.
Courtesy, Arroyo Trading Post.

Two Grey Hills style weaving. Woven by Sherman. 58" x 35". Courtesy, Arroyo Trading Post.

Standard weaving with natural wools, the design closely associated with Two Grey Hills style. 24" x 60". Courtesy, Keams Canyon Arts and Crafts.

Two Grey Hills style weaving of handspun yarn. Woven by Betty Tom. 49½" x 32". Courtesy, Turquoise Lady.

Four-in-one weaving with Two Grey Hills styles in variations. Woven by Lillie Taylor, 1977. 70" x 72". Courtesy, Private Collection.

A very recent variation of the Two Grey Hills design has developed a little east of the old post site near Burnham, New Mexico. Here, artist and painter Bobby Johnson worked with a few local weavers to design pictorial elements into the geometric designs, still with primarily natural wools. The addition of pottery, feathers, the ceremonial Yei figures and flute player Kokopele, and other pictorial elements give these weavings very distinctive designs. It will be interesting to watch the development of this style.

Burnham variation of Two Grey Hills style, designed by Bobby Johnson, 1989. Woven by Linda Bitsuie. 38" x 29". Courtesy, Arroyo Trading Post.

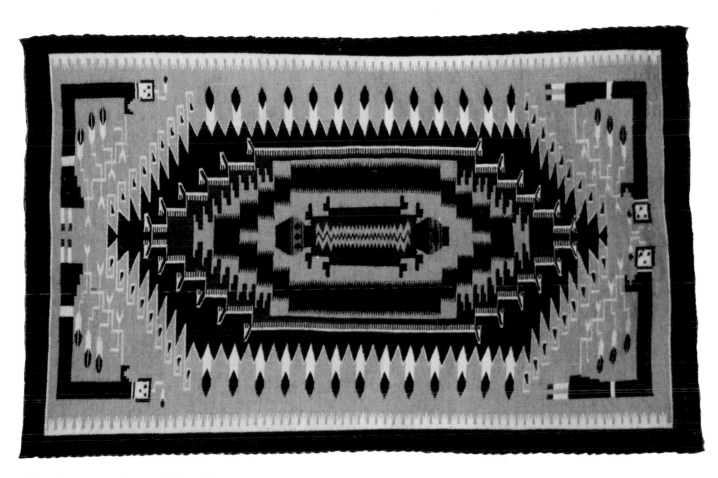

Burnham variation of Two Grey Hills style, designed by Bobby Johnson, 1989. Woven by Linda Bltsuie. 46" x 29". Courtesy, Arroyo Trading Post.

Burnham variation of Two Grey Hills style, designed by Bobby Johnson, 1989. Woven by Esther Bitsuie. 40" x 31". Courtesy, Arroyo Trading Post.

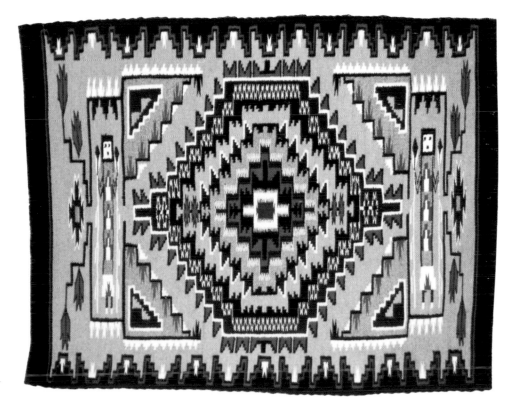

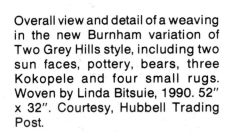

Overall view and detail of a weaving in the new Burnham variation of Two Grey Hills style, including two sun faces, pottery, bears, three Kokopele and four small rugs. Woven by Linda Bitsuie, 1990. 52" x 32". Courtesy, Hubbell Trading Post.

Opposite page:
Mountains and desert, the extremes within Navajo lands.

Teec Nos Pos

The name Teec Nos Pos comes from the Navajo language meaning "a circle of cotton-woods" which described the original site of the trading post by the same name which has dealt with weavers in the land around the Four Corners area where Utah, Colorado, New Mexico and Arizona meet.

The style of weaving has developed since the early decades of this century with apparently Persian rug design elements whose introduction to the Navajo is not fully known. Among the Teec Nos Pos characteristics is a wide border with contrasting T-, H-, and L-shaped figures. They may be traced to the introduction of commercial blankets, since the T-shaped design in borders has a precedent in commercial blankets like those introduced by the Hudson's Bay Company to Tlingit basketmakers in the Pacific Northwest. (Turnbaugh and Turnbaugh, *Indian Baskets,* p. viii.) Bright, commercial and synthetically dyed wool makes up the central geometric designs which sometimes have contrasting outlines woven in the raised outline technique.

Teec Nos Pos style weaving with green border. Woven by Lucille Begay, 1990. 68" x 47". Courtesy, Foutz Trading Company.

Teec Nos Pos style weaving, natural and synthetic dyed wool. Woven by Cleo Blackwater. Courtesy, Foutz Trading Company.

Teec Nos Pos style weaving. Woven by Daisy King. Courtesy, Foutz Trading Company.

Teec Nos Pos style weaving with colorful design on a white background. Woven by Mary Begay, 1990. 51″ x 38″. Courtesy, Hogback Trading Post.

Teec Nos Pos style weaving, 1990. Courtesy, Hogback Trading Post.

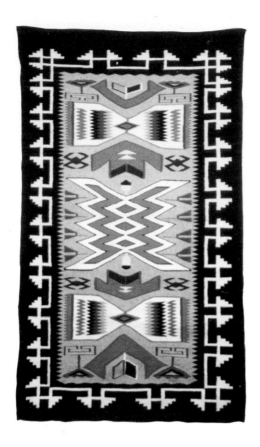

Teec Nos Pos style weaving with brown border and colorful central design. Woven by Mary Poyer. 37" x 64". Courtesy, Hubbell Trading Post.

Teec Nos Pos style weaving. Woven by Maxine White, 1989. 55" x 48". Courtesy, Foutz Trading Company.

Teec Nos Pos style weaving, geometric, circa 1980. Courtesy, Dennehotso Collection.

Teec Nos Pos style, multi-geometric weaving. Woven by Phebe Nelson, 1990. 68" x 49½". Courtesy, Foutz Trading Company.

Teec Nos Pos style weaving with four diamonds. Woven by Molly Benally. Courtesy, Foutz Trading Company.

Small geometric weaving in Teec Nos Pos style with dark pink center. Woven by Ruby Poyer, 1990. 21" x 15". Courtesy, Foutz Trading Company.

Teec Nos Pos style weaving with central diamonds and two figured borders. Woven by Daisey Joe. 45″ x 28″. Courtesy, Foutz Trading Company.

Teec Nos Pos weaving in natural and synthetic grey wool. Woven by Darlen Kee, 1990. 65″ x 99″. Courtesy, Hogback Trading Post.

Teec Nos Pos style weaving with red diamonds pattern. Woven by Sadie and Darleen Kee, 1990. 89½″ x 56″. Courtesy, Hogback Trading Post.

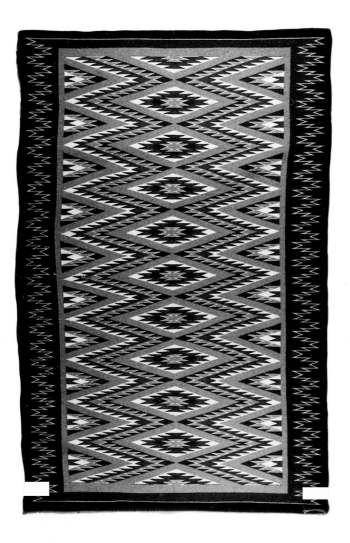

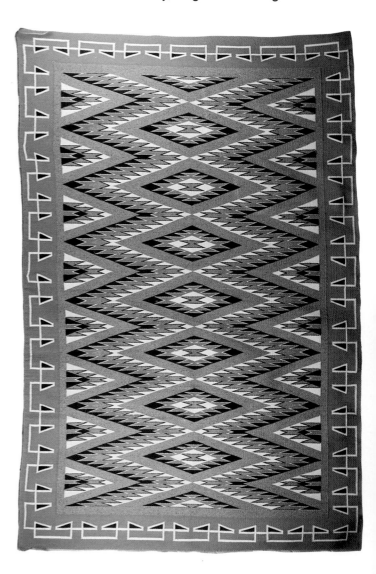

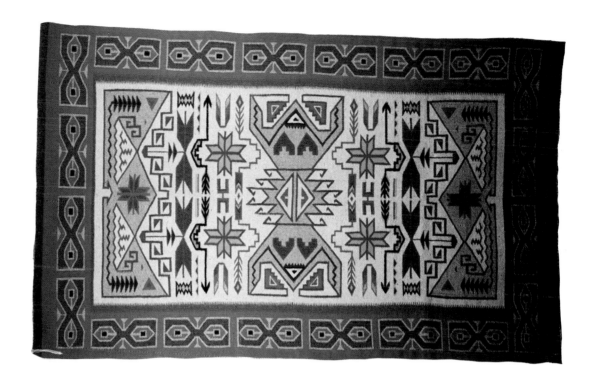

Teec Nos Pos style weaving with pink geometric design. Woven by Sarah George, Burntwater, 1990. 79″ x 49½″. Courtesy, Foutz Trading Company.

Two nearly identical Teec Nos Pos style weavings. The subtle color and design variations proclaim the clever versatility of this weaver. Woven by Mary Lee Begay, 1990. Each 35″ x 60″. Courtesy, Hubbell Trading Post.

Small Teec Nos Pos style weaving with exceptionally fine detail. Woven by Gloria Cambridge, 1989. 33" x 27". Courtesy, Foutz Trading Company.

Teec Nos Pos style weaving with an unusual border and uncharacteristic Ganado style dark red and grey design. Woven by Nora Young, 1989. 57" x 39". Courtesy, Foutz Trading Company.

Teec Nos Pos style runner woven with raised outline. Woven by Florence Scott, Sanders. 31" x 91". Courtesy, Hubbell Trading Post.

Teec Nos Pos style geometric weaving with two diamonds in raised outline technique. Woven by Maretta Littleben, 1990. 27″ x 20¼″. Courtesy, Shiprock Trading Company.

Teec Nos Pos style weaving in raised outline technique. Woven by Sally Yazzie, 1989. 59″ x 41″. Courtesy, Foutz Trading Company.

Teec Nos Pos style weaving with raised outline technique, 1989. 60″ x 82″. Courtesy, Keams Canyon Arts and Crafts.

Western Reservation

At the western edges of Navajo lands, in remote canyons and along impassable trails, clusters of inhabitants live nearly as their ancestors did a century and more ago. Away from much contact with white people or their technologies, weaving has remained traditional in many respects while utilizing commercial yarns regularly.

Storm pattern

Here a common type of weaving design is now called the Storm Pattern. Its origin is uncertain, for some feel the design is derived from sacred markings, while others say it was a trader's idea, and that any symbolism has been applied to it by a romantic public. Nevertheless, the storm pattern is a distinctive design of a central rectangle with four lines extending from its corners to four rectangles at the corners of the weaving. The rectangles may be filled with geometric or even pictorial designs. The use of commercial yarns brings a wide spectrum of color to these weavings, yet black and white are predominant.

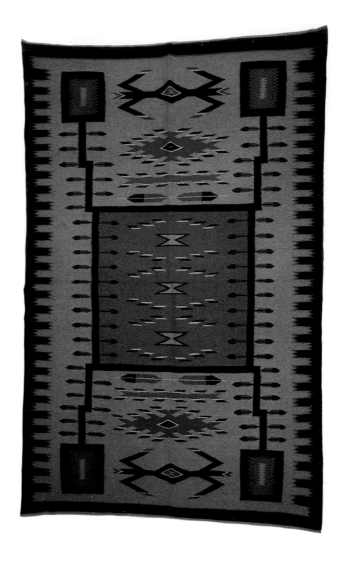

Western reservation style storm pattern design. Woven by Lillian Begay, 1973. Courtesy, Private Collection.

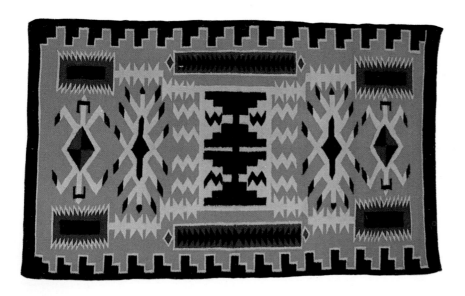

Storm pattern design from the Western Reservation area with yellow background. Woven by Edna Joe. Courtesy, Private Collection.

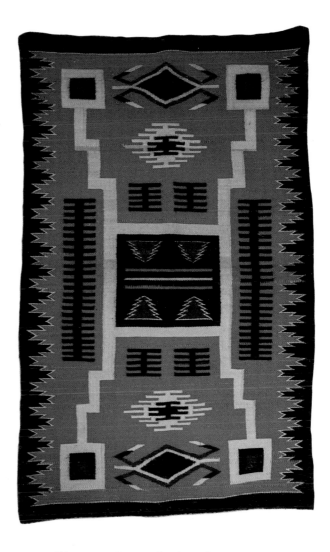

Storm pattern design weaving from the Western Reservation area. Woven by Pauline T. Nez, 1973. Courtesy, Dennehotso Collection.

Storm pattern design from the Western Reservation area with yellow background. Woven by Helen Watchman. Courtesy, Dennehotso Collection.

Storm pattern design from the Western Reservation area. Woven by Lita Ann Feather. Courtesy, Private Collection.

Raised outline

Basic geometric designs frequently woven in the Western Reservation area include variations on squares, diamonds and triangles. To highlight the figures, some weavers outline the important designs with a contrasting color, and these designs are known as Outline designs.

A special weaving technique is used to further enhance Outline designs to make a Raised Outline style. In these weavings, the weaver uses a weft thread of a different color over two warps instead of the usual one. This technique produces a higher stitch on one side of the pattern.

Geometric weaving in plain stitch from the Western Reservation area, circa 1970. Courtesy, Dennehotso Collection.

Geometric weaving with commercial yarn and an Outlined design, made in the Western Reservation area. Woven by Joanna Goat, 1969. 24" x 36". Courtesy, Dennehotso Collection.

Raised outline geometric weaving from the Western Reservation area, 1989. 44" x 31". Courtesy, Keams Canyon Trading Post.

Raised outline storm pattern weaving. Woven by Doris Haskan, 1975. Courtesy, Dennehotso Collection.

Western Reservation style, raised outline storm pattern weaving with grey background. Courtesy, Dennehotso Collection.

Raised outline storm pattern weaving in commercial yarn. Woven by Doris Haskan, 1960. 25" x 40". Courtesy, Dennehotso Collection.

Shiprock Pictorials

In the remote northern part of the Navajo lands, from about Shiprock, New Mexico west to Kayenta, Arizona, weavers have devised for themselves and been encouraged by traders to "paint a picture" with their weaving. Animals, birds, words, landscape designs, even humorous and symbolic designs appear, usually with a border, and in a variety of commercial and analin dyed wools. The pictorial images are delightful and fresh representations of Navajo scenes of daily life, and some even of designs derived from ceremonial religious images.

Eagle and rabbit pictorial weaving. Woven by Nellie Tapaho, 1990. 25" x 19". Courtesy, O'Grady's Old Town Trading Company.

Miniature pictorial landscape weaving. Woven by Betty Belin, circa 1980. 9½" x 8". Courtesy, Private Collection.

Eagle with flags pictorial weaving. Woven by Sadie Ross, 1976. 24½" x 22". Courtesy, Foutz Trading Company.

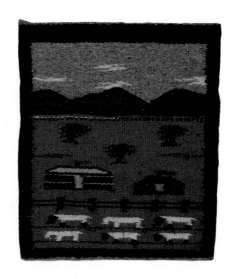

Pictorial weaving of bears. Woven by Jane Gray, 1989. 25" x 27". Courtesy, Schiffer Publishing Collection.

Pictorial weaving of a ceremonial corn plant tree of life with birds. Woven by Elyn Tunney. 61" x 42½". Courtesy, Foutz Trading Company.

Small pictorial weaving of a landscape with two trucks. Woven by Charalott Begay, 1990. 26¾" x 19½". Courtesy, Foutz Trading Company.

Pictorial weaving of a landscape with windmill and water trough. Woven by Louise Van Winkle, 1990. 28" x 37". Courtesy, Shiprock Trading Company.

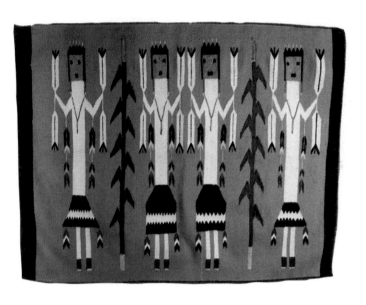

Pictorial weaving of a ceremonial sandpainting design depicting four sacred buffalo. Woven by Rita Gilmore, 1990. 34" x 38". Courtesy, Hubbell Trading Post.

Pictorial weaving of ceremonial Yei dancers and corn plants, 1990. 30" x 37¼". Courtesy, Turquoise Lady.

Miniature pictorial rug with four corn plants and a maiden. 3½" x 4¼". Courtesy, Palms Trading Company.

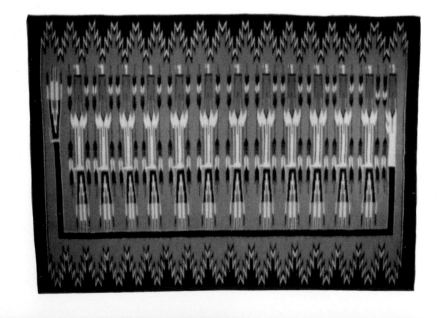

Ceremonial sandpainting design weaving of stylized Yei. Woven by Elizabeth Atcitty, circa 1985. Courtesy, Foutz Trading Company.

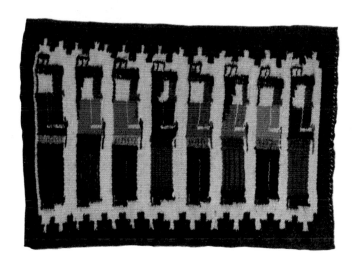

Miniature pictorial weaving of Yei dancers, 1989. 12½″ x 18″. Courtesy, Foutz Trading Company.

Miniature pictorial weaving with four Yei figures. 9½″ x 7¼″. Courtesy, Private Collection.

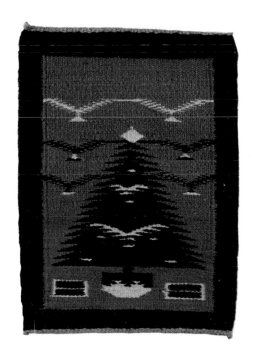

Small woven pictorial mat with decorated Christmas design. Woven by Charlotte Begay, 1989. 14¾″ x 10½″. Courtesy, Schiffer Publishing Collection.

Four-in-one weaving of designs in a figured background surrounding individual squares. The squares contain a pictorial, Two Grey Hills, Teec Nos Pos and Storm Pattern regional designs, all in vegetal dyed wool. Woven by Eunice Mason, 1978. 48″ x 56″. Courtesy, Private Collection on permanent loan to Ohio University.

SPECIAL PURPOSE AND FANCY WEAVES

Saddle Blankets

Still woven for their original function are saddle blankets which come with a rainbow of colors, usually arranged in stripes. Single size (30" x 30") and double size (30" x 60"), they are woven to wear well under a saddle, and oftn have ornamental fringe and tassels. As pick-up trucks and automobiles continue to infiltrate even the remote areas of the Navajo lands, these weavings may become obsolete.

Double size saddle blanket of aqua stripes. Woven by Cecilia Calomity, Shonto, Arizona. 62" x 31". Courtesy, Hubbell Trading Company.

Single size saddle blanket. Woven by Edna Joe, 1973. Courtesy, Private Collection.

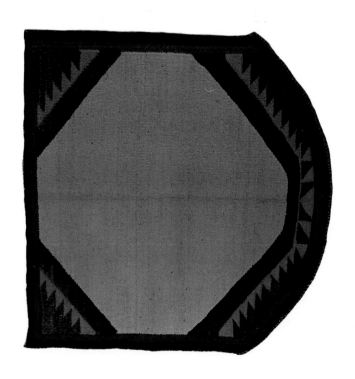

Single size saddle blanket shaped for a close fit. Courtesy, Private Collection.

Single size saddle blanket. Woven by Katy Furcap, Chinle, Arizona. 30″ x 30″. Courtesy, Hubbell Trading Post.

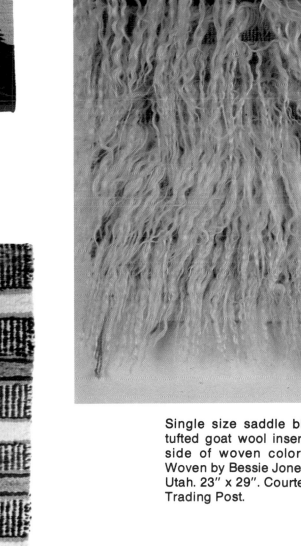

Single size saddle blanket with tufted goat wool inserted on one side of woven colorful stripes. Woven by Bessie Jones, Blanding, Utah. 23″ x 29″. Courtesy, Hubbell Trading Post.

Single size saddle blanket of striped bands. 30″ x 32″. Courtesy, Keams Canyon Trading Post

Round

In the 1970s a different shape appeared from weavers, round mats woven in Ganado style colors and designs, using a wagon wheel as a loom frame.

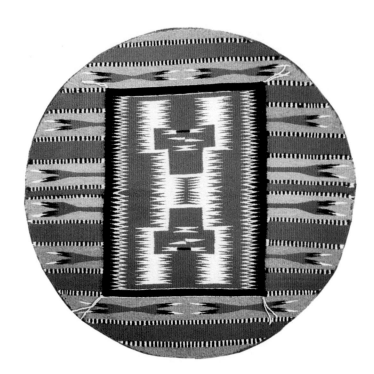

Round weaving with storm pattern mat woven into a banded design. Woven by Lillie Hosteen. 41″ diameter. Courtesy, Hogback Trading Post.

Round weaving of Ganado red and grey design. Woven by Lillie Hosteen. About 40″ diameter. Courtesy, Hogback Trading Post.

Round weaving of brown Ganado geometric design. Woven by Wilson Begay. 20″ diameter. Courtesy, Kiva Indian Trading Post.

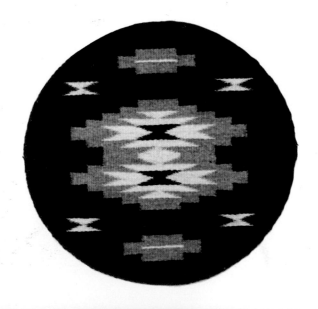

Round weaving of Ganado red design. Woven by Barbara Begay. 15″ diameter. Courtesy, Foutz Trading Company.

Double Weaves

Only truly gifted and daring weavers attempt to make double weavings where diamond twill patterns have reverse colors on the front and back sides.

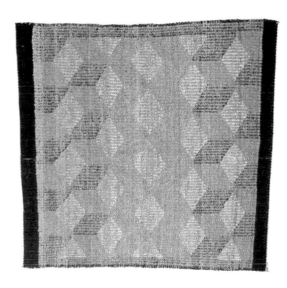

Double weave saddle blanket, geometric black twill pattern. Woven by Oliver's old sister, Old Maud. Courtesy, Private Collection.

Double weave saddle blanket of vegetal dyed twill pattern. Woven by Lucy Wilson, 1971. 30" x 31". Courtesy, Private Collection on permanent loan to Ohio University.

Two-faced

Intricately constructed weavings with entirely different designs on the front and back sides are known as Two-Faced weavings. Because of the extra wool carried to make each design, these are quite heavy. Few weavers attempt two-faced projects, so very few are ever available.

Two-faced Chinle style saddle blanket with diamond design and colored bands on one side and plain straight weave on the reverse. 55" x 26½". Courtesy, Private Collection on permanent loan to Ohio University.

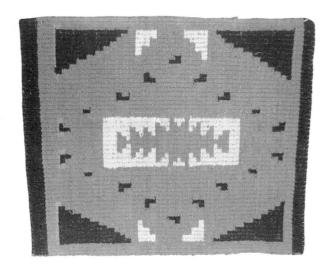

Two-faced saddle blanket with stripes on one side and geometric pattern on the reverse. Woven by Louise Francis. Courtesy, Private Collection.

Multiples

Ambitious weavers capable of designing more than one regional design once in a while make a multiple patterned weaving to demonstrate their skill. Most of these are Four-In-One designs, but occasionally there are Five-, Six-, Eight-, Nine-In-One and more. These are among the rarest Navajo weavings of the contemporary types.

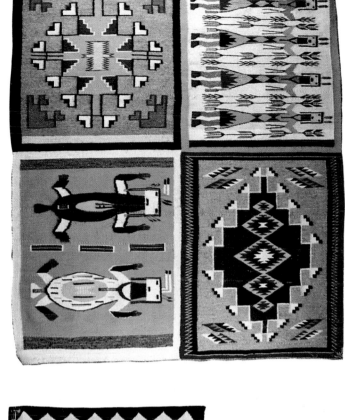

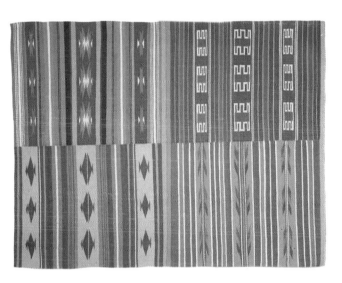

Beautiful multiple Four-In-One weaving in Wide Ruins style, vegetal dyed stripes. Woven by Susie Small, 1979. 49½" x 39". Courtesy, Private Collection on permanent loan to Ohio University.

Top right:
Multiple Four-In-One weaving including a Pictorial Yei, Western Reservation outline, Ganado, and Pictorial sandpainting (Mother Earth and Father sky) designs. Woven by Mary Yazzie. 54" x 45". Courtesy, Turquoise Lady.

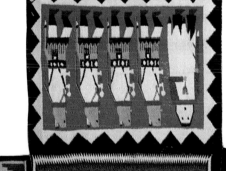

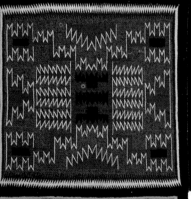

Multiple Five-In-One weaving in a cross shape with Two Grey Hills, Pictorial Yei bei chei dancers, Storm Pattern, Pictorial Yei figures with corn stalk and Ganado style designs. Woven by Alice Benally. 59½". Courtesy, Private Collection on permanent loan to Ohio University.

Multiple Nine-In-One weaving in Ganado style. Woven by Shirley Lopez. 60" x 41½". Courtesy, Hogback Trading Post.

Multiple weaving with sixteen different regional styles: Outside, Wide Ruins. Inside, Burntwater. Left row from top, Burntwater, Wide Ruins, Ganado, Saddle cloth, Pictorial Yei bi chei, Old Ganado, and Storm Pattern. Right row from top, Pictorial sandpainting, Crystal, Two Grey Hills, Double weave twill, Ganado (Klagetoh), Chinle, and Pictorial birds. Woven by Sarah Begay, Whitecone, Arizona, 1990. 96" x 60". Courtesy, McGee's Beyond Indian Tradition Gallery.

Four-In-One Burntwater style weaving. Woven by Lillie Taylor, 1977. 70" x 72". Courtesy, Private Collection on permanent loan to Ohio University.

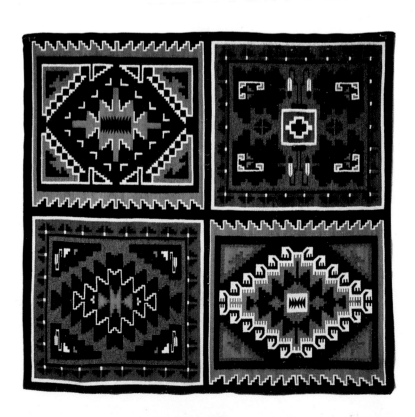